A Cloud of Sail

Maritime Paintings by

J. STEVEN DEWS

Written by Louise A. Felstead

Dedication

We dedicate this book to

John Paul, Hollie, Rosanna, Thomas, Savanna, Christopher, Sam, Alex

Louise A. Felstead

Louise Felstead has been associated with the yachting world for over twenty years. She grew up in Lymington, a bustling sailing community on the south coast of England, where she began an exciting nautical career. Working on large yachts and based for various periods in the Mediterranean, Canada, USA and Japan, Louise had the opportunity to sail and work on some of the most extraordinary vessels in the most exotic places. In 1999 her job as shore manager of the 'J' Class yacht, *Velsheda*, took Louise to Antigua Race Week where she met the renowned marine artist J. Steven Dews. Louise's passion for the artist's works led to their collaboration on this book.

Acknowledgements

Oliver Swann, of the Tryon & Swann Gallery, David Roe and Lucy McDowell of Rosenstiel's Fine Art Publishers, Glenn Dunn and Juliet Ashworth.

Thanks are offered to the following from Steven for the inspiration their work has given him

Artists
John Ward, 1798–1849, Thomas J. Somerscales of Hull, 1842–1927, Montague Dawson, 1895–1973, Joseph Mallord William Turner, 1775–1851, and Charles Napier Hemy, 1841–1917.

Writers
Basil Lubbock, John Irving, Ian Dear, Eric Johnston, Occomore Sibbick, and Thomas W. Lawson.

Photographer
Beken of Cowes

Paintings and Illustrations Copyright © 2001 J. Steven Dews
Text Copyright © 2001 Louise A. Felstead

First published in the UK in 2001
by Sweet Lake, an imprint of Airlife Publishing Ltd

British Library Cataloguing-in-Publication Data
  A catalogue record for this book
  is available from the British Library

ISBN 1 903984 00 9

The information in this book is true and complete to the best of our knowledge. The Publisher disclaims any liability incurred in connection with the use of this data or specific details.

Typeset by Rowland Phototypesetting Limited, Bury St Edmunds, Suffolk
Printed in Hong Kong

Sweet Lake
an imprint of Airlife Publishing Ltd
101 Longden Road, Shrewsbury, SY3 9EB, England
E-mail: sweetlakebooks.com
Website: www.sweetlakebooks.com

Contents

Introduction

This introduction could read like the numerous newspaper and magazine articles that have been written about Steven over the twenty-five years of his career as a professional artist. It could tell you that he was born in Hull in 1949, that he failed his art 'A' level and that he walked out on a Fine Arts degree after only a few weeks because he was so disillusioned by the teaching methods. Instead I want to explore the inner man: how his remarkable talent developed; what motivates him and what inspires him to produce such perfectly executed paintings. As a child, Steven's all-consuming passion was not for fire engines or toy soldiers but ships, sailing ships. Even now, he recalls as a five-year-old having his painting of a ship displayed on the wall of his classroom for a parents' evening at St John's Infant School. The memory jars because the teacher had hung his painting before he had finished the rigging and he was furious.

Perhaps there was a degree of inherited interest in ships and the sea. Steven's family had owned keelboats for many generations. These were square-sail rigged barges that traded along the Yorkshire coast. His grandfather had served in the Merchant Navy for twenty-five years before being appointed assistant harbour-master in the busy port of Hull, Yorkshire. He regaled his young grandson with stories of his exploits at sea, telling him about his involvement in smuggling whisky into America during prohibition and of the frequent gun battles between the smugglers and the authorities. Steven's love of the maritime world flourished. While other young adults were turning their attentions to new experiences, Steven was absorbed in his hobbies of drawing, painting and building model ships. Instead of partying with his peers he could be found engrossed in maritime reference books or studying the art and artefacts in the Hull Maritime Museum.

After careful analysis of technical drawings, Steven was able to build scale replicas of the ships that he admired using scraps of timber and other materials that he could scavenge. The sails were hand-sewn and dyed in cold tea to resemble the authentic colour of aged canvas. The rigging was made from fishing line and electrical wire, begged from his stepfather, who taught marine electronics in the local college. His passion extended beyond the models. He longed to experience the sensation of propulsion under sail and, at the age of fourteen, he set about designing and building a land-yacht. With experimentation, modification and the redesigning of three land-yachts, he perfected his ultimate machine.

He sailed for hours along the lanes of the flat countryside around his home in Yorkshire. He planned a five-mile route, allowing for the prevailing wind, which followed a circuitous course without the need to manhandle his yacht or tack in the narrow lanes.

He may have suffered the ignominy of failing his art 'A' level, but Steven already excelled in metalwork and technical drawing. At the age of eighteen, his brilliant mastery of design precision and technical detail was beginning to show in his art. Coupled with his growing knowledge of sailing, these skills formed the basis for the extraordinary artistic talent that is the hallmark of his work today. So by his late teens we see a young man already imbued with a detailed knowledge of ships and the sea, an eye for technical detail and a marked skill with a pencil and brush. The discipline of a three-year technical graphic design and illustration course was all that was needed to hone his craft.

By the age of twenty-one, Steven had all the skills he required to pursue his dream of becoming a marine artist. In fact, in the arrogance of youth he would tell those close to him that he aspired to be 'the best marine artist, living or dead'. Steven's journey to this elevated rank was not easy. Family pressure to 'get a proper job' and the need to earn enough money to survive led this shy and unassuming young man into a job as a car salesman in Hull. Dressed in the only suit that he has ever owned, he reluctantly learnt some valuable lessons about sales and customer relationships. He next worked for various lengths of time as a milkman, a travelling sales rep and a caravan salesman – but he never stopped painting. When travelling, Steven could be found kneeling on the floor of his dingy motel room by night using his bed as an easel to support his canvases. To this day, those years have left Steven with an ability to exist on very little sleep.

Meanwhile Steven studied the works of artists such as John Ward, J.A.C. Spurling, Montague Dawson and Turner. He tried to blend the technical accuracy of Ward and Spurling with the spirit of Dawson, while adapting the use of light and atmospherics perfected by Turner.

At the age of twenty-four, with very little money, Steven travelled to London with two of his paintings. One was, by his own admission, a close copy of a painting by one of his mentors, J.A.C. Spurling, but the other was an original composition of the fully rigged ship *Waitmate*, which was built in Sunderland in 1874 and carried passengers to the colonies. He had calculated their value based on the average weekly wage of a Yorkshire docker.

Steven proudly presented them to a gallery in the belief that they would be snapped up, but the gallery owner dismissed them, telling him to take his pictures and go back to Yorkshire. Undaunted, Steven approached a gallery in his home-town. The proprietor immediately recognised one painting as a copy but was impressed by the other and purchased it.

Steven trailed his rejected painting around town until he found a small gallery willing to display it, and indeed, the owner gave it pride of place in the window. That night the gallery burnt to the ground. Seventeen years later, at a dinner party, Steven fell into conversation with an insurance assessor who mentioned that he owned one of his paintings. To Steven's amazement, it turned out to be the ill-fated painting believed to have been lost in the gallery fire. However, the meager insurance payment received by Steven at the time had been enough to fund the purchase of canvas and oils that became his first exhibited works. Steven took the fate of the plagiarised work as an omen and never again copied another artist.

The sale of his first picture was the only encouragement Steven needed to take the plunge and begin painting full time. The first two years proved a bitter struggle. A sympathetic friend gave him the use of a remote, semi-derelict farm cottage on the flat lands of Sunk Island. Here, in this cold, damp place, he set up his first studio. Steven comments that although the cottage was far from ideal it had two distinct advantages: it was totally peaceful, apart from the resident cockerel, and it afforded him wide, uninterrupted views of the sky. The cloud formations and light that he observed in those early days helped him to understand and interpret the relationship between the sky and the sea. The methods he developed then, to give depth to his work by the use of shadow and light, are still an important element in his paintings.

Two years later he had produced enough paintings to warrant an exhibition. In 1976 he staged a one-man show in a local art gallery. It was an immediate sell-out, all eighteen paintings were sold on the opening night, and led to a further seventeen commissions. Unfortunately, Steven's naïveté meant that he did not profit from his debut show personally. In 1978 Steven staged his second show in San Francisco. Six of his works were hung and every one of them sold within the first few hours. His international reputation was quickly established.

Over the next few years he was invited to undertake many prestigious commissions. One of the earlier commissions was a set of twelve paintings for AMOCO. The paintings were reproduced in a calendar as well as being published as a limited-edition print series. AMOCO allowed the paintings to form part of an exhibition that was to travel around Britain raising money for the Mary Rose Trust. This charity, whose patron was HRH the Prince of Wales, had been formed to raise the Tudor warship, Mary Rose, from the seabed off Portsmouth where she had lain since 1545. The exhibition exposed Steven's work to a wide audience and raised his profile considerably.

Steven's work is predominantly privately commissioned, but he has also been invited to undertake some very exciting projects. In 1986 he was appointed the official artist for the British America's Cup challenge team in Perth. He was commissioned to produce two paintings that were to be published as limited-edition prints. The proceeds from the sales were to help fund the British challenge. Then in 1988 Steven was awarded another great honour when he was commissioned by the Maritime Services Board of the Australian Government to record the re-enactment of the First Fleet's arrival in Botany Bay and the bicentennial celebrations in Sydney Harbour.

In 1995 Steven was again awarded another prestigious commission. He was asked to create a painting to record the one hundred and fiftieth anniversary of the formation of the New York Yacht Club. Part of the celebrations was a parade of members' yachts, which Steven captured with great skill on canvas. Steven's career goes from strength to strength, and the arrogant dream of his youth to become the 'best marine artist living or dead' may well become a reality. Steven's enthusiasm for his subject has not diminished: 'I can remember the emotions that were evoked in me when I first sailed my wooden land-yacht up and down the lanes of Sunk Island in Yorkshire. My heart still beats faster when I stand on a deck and look up at a perfectly trimmed sail. I must have painted hundreds of sails and miles of rigging but the form and the function of those vessels I have painted still fascinate and entrance me. I feel the perfect painting is still inside me. If I ever achieve it I think I will stop painting. You know, I somehow don't think that will ever happen.'

America's Cup

America

This is one of Steven's earliest yachting paintings and depicts the schooner *America* in the Solent during her visit to Britain in the summer of 1851. *America* was the response to a challenge set by the Royal Yacht Squadron as part of the celebrations in the year of the Great Exhibition – 'A contest of speed, between pleasure vessels, open to all comers'. Three members of the newly formed New York Yacht Club, the then Commodore John Stevens, his brother Edwin and George Schuyler, answered the challenge and ordered the building of a 140-ton New York pilot boat. The vessel was to be designed by the young but very talented George Steers and built in W.H. Brown's yard under the total supervision of Steers. Such was the confidence of Steers and Brown that they would produce the fastest yacht afloat, it was proposed to the owners that if *America* was beaten by a British yacht of the same size they could reject her.

When *America* sailed down the Solent towards Cowes on 1 August 1851, escorted by the cutter *Laverock*, everyone was there to see. The *London Times* likened the British yachtsmen's reaction to that which 'the appearance of a sparrow hawk on the horizon creates among a flock of wood pigeons'. The obvious fact that *America*'s speed was far superior to that of any British yacht meant that it was some time before an English yacht owner would come forward to defend the Cup. Eventually, Mr R. Stephenson bravely put his yacht *Titania* forward to race against *America*.

The Royal Yacht Squadron race for the One Hundred Guineas Cup took place on Friday 22 August. The race was around the Isle of Wight, outside the Nab Tower. There was no handicap, so the first yacht over the finish line was the winner. Although eighteen yachts came to the start, when the gun went off at 10.00 a.m. only fifteen yachts were away. *Titania*, *Fernande* and *Stella* failed to start.

America worked her way through the fleet and well into the lead, and although *Aurora* put up a brave fight she could not catch the American schooner. *America* came home to great applause and cheers from the waiting crowds, completing the race in eight hours and thirty-four minutes, and the Royal Yacht Squadron Cup became the *America*'s Cup.

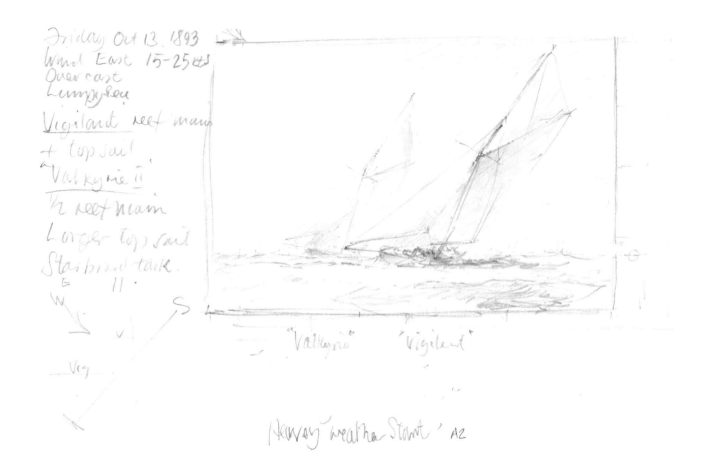

Heavy Weather Start

*U*nder the new, more detailed and stringent Deed of Gift, drawn up by the New York Yacht Club in 1857, all races were to be on the ocean, over thirty miles, with alternating triangular and windward–leeward courses. The new Deed also set out very clear guidelines as to the permissible dimensions of any future challengers. The Deed of Gift caused some criticism, and it was not until 1893, and after some negotiations with the New York Yacht Club, that Lord Dunraven challenged the Americans with his Watson-designed *Valkyrie II*.

The American defence came from New York banker C. Oliver Iselin with his Herreshoff-designed *Vigilant*. *Vigilant* was the first

of a long line of *America*'s Cup defenders designed by Herreshoff. She was a centreboard, gaff cutter, and required a crew of seventy men, not to handle the yacht but to add stability to an extremely light vessel, which was almost impossible to steer. She also had a very complicated rig.

Valkyrie II proved to be a faster yacht and it was bad luck rather than boat speed that lost the British the Cup. *Vigilant* won by a mere forty seconds on corrected time. This was the most exciting *America*'s Cup challenge yet witnessed and gave the British great hope for the future.

Columbia and *Shamrock* off Rhode Island, 1899

The inspiration for this painting came from an old photograph taken from the deck of *Columbia* looking aft at *Shamrock* with her vast mainsail boomed out and spinnaker pole set. Sir Thomas Lipton, aboard *Shamrock*, tried in vain to lessen the gap between the two yachts by blanketing *Columbia*'s sails with *Shamrock*'s own huge spread.

Although Lipton sailed home across the Atlantic having lost the race, he had won the hearts of the Americans with his kindly, sportsmanlike behaviour. He had done much to smooth the strained relations that had developed between Britain and America after the trouble caused by the outspoken Earl of Dunraven during the previous challenge in 1895.

Lipton came from a poor background. Born in Scotland to Irish parents he emigrated to America as a youth, working for some time in a New York grocery store, where he learnt his trade. At the age of nineteen Lipton returned to Scotland and opened his first store. From these humble beginnings grew a commercial empire that stretched around the globe.

The *Shamrock* of the 1899 challenge was the first of five that Lipton owned during his yachting career. The last of his *Shamrocks* is still racing, with some success, in regattas around the world.

Endeavour and *Rainbow*

The challenge for the 1934 *America*'s Cup came in September 1933 from Mr Thomas Sopwith via the Royal Yacht Squadron. Vanderbilt took up the challenge and formed a syndicate of seventeen people to put together a defence – the result was *Rainbow*. Designed by Starling Burgess and built by Herreshoff, *Rainbow* was possibly one of the prettiest American 'J' Class yachts.

Sopwith's *Endeavour* was to prove the most serious challenger for the Cup the Americans had had to face so far. She was thought by the commentators of the day to be a faster yacht. She was fitted with all the 'state of the art' technology of the time and a magnificent suit of sails, including Sopwith's revolutionary new quadrilateral jib. However, an amateur crew and bad tactical decisions handicapped *Endeavour*'s performance on the water.

The series of races got off to a poor start with disagreements between the opposing teams. There was much wrangling over *Rainbow*'s winch and interior fittings and the acrimony continued on the water. In the fourth race Sopwith attempted to luff *Rainbow* but was forced to bear away to avoid a collision. Sopwith protested, but due to a bureaucratic error, his protest was rejected. Had Sopwith's protest been accepted, it might have altered the overall result and *Endeavour* might have won the Cup.

A5. Jumping the Gun

Jumping the Gun

Following his near success with *Endeavour*, in the 1934 *America*'s Cup, Thomas Sopwith decided to build a new yacht to challenge again in 1937. *Endeavour II*, designed by Nicholson, was launched in the summer of 1936. Trail races in the Solent that summer between the two *Endeavours* showed the new yacht to have superior speed. This fact led the Americans to realise that they would have to design and build a new defender if they were to hold onto the Cup.

The collaboration between the designers Olin Stephens and Starling Burgess produced the most radical 'J' Class yet seen for Vanderbilt's defence. They had pushed the design parameters to the limits, with startling results. *Ranger* was certainly not the

prettiest of yachts with her weight-saving, bluff bow but her speed was extraordinary. During the summer of her launch she competed in thirty-four races, conceding only two. She appeared to all to be unbeatable.

Vanderbilt's *Ranger* started late in both the first and the second races of the Cup series but with her blistering speed she beat *Endeavour* by more than fifteen minutes in each race. *Ranger* took the third race, and clever tactics from Vanderbilt at the start of the fourth race put *Endeavour* over the line early, giving her a one and a half minute disadvantage against the defender. Although Sopwith fought back valiantly it was in vain and the *America*'s Cup stayed, once again, on American soil.

Australia II tacks for the line – *America*'s Cup 1983

The Americans finally lost their 132-year grip on the Cup in 1983. This year was Alan Bond's fifth challenge, and the Australian team knew from early on in the campaign that they had a winning boat with its revolutionary winged keel. *Australia II* was designed by the late Ben Lexcen and skippered by John Bertrand. Her supremacy on the water became obvious during the selection trials and the Louis Vuitton Cup. Many felt that *Australia II* was the fastest and most manoeuvrable 12-metre yacht that they had ever seen race in the waters off Rhode Island. The Americans questioned the legality of the fin on the keel of *Australia II* but decided to give the Australians the benefit of the doubt and maintain their reputation as sportsmen. This situation put Dennis Connor with his defending yacht *Liberty* in a weakened position, and although the Americans put up a valiant fight they lost the Cup in the final race of the seven-race series. In this painting we see Bertrand taking *Australia II* on the final tack to the line and victory!

Crossing Ahead

After the 1983 ignominy of being the first American to lose the *America*'s Cup, Dennis Conner, with single-minded determination, set out to reclaim the Cup and bring it back to his home country.

The sailing conditions of the shark-infested, rough waters off Fremantle, the Cup's new Western Australian home, were very different from the traditional *America*'s Cup race-courses off Newport, Rhode Island. Conner therefore had to find a training venue that would have similar conditions to those in Fremantle. He took his team and boats to Hawaii. Using his old yacht *Liberty* as a bench mark, he acquired the 1983 yacht *Spirit of America* and rebuilt her. She became the first *Stars and Stripes*. He then went on to develop three more *Stars and Stripes*, each one faster and more powerful than its predecessor. In 1987 Conner won the Louis Vuitton Cup and the right to challenge for the *America*'s Cup. During the *America*'s Cup series Conner demolished Kevin Parry's tough *Kookaburra* defence in four straight wins.

Stars and Stripes

*D*ennis Conner aboard *Stars and Stripes* won the right to challenge for the 1987 *America*'s Cup (and Ian Murray aboard *Kookaburra* to defend), in the Louis Vuitton races off Fremantle in Western Australia. This painting depicts the climax of the *America*'s Cup as Dennis Conner 'outsails' Kevin Parry's *Kookaburra* to win back the trophy he lost to *Australia II* in 1983. *Stars and Stripes* dips under the stern of *Kookaburra*, sailing past the Australian yacht to leeward. This clearly illustrated the American yacht's superior boat speed and they never looked back! Dennis Conner proved himself to be the finest 12-metre skipper in the world. He beat Australia on their home waters, which are much more boisterous than the gentle conditions to be found in Newport, Rhode Island.

KA 15 *Kookaburra*, designed by John Swarbrick and her skipper Ian Murray, sailed under the flag of the Royal Perth Yacht Club. US-55 *Stars and Stripes*, designed by Britton Chance, Bruce Nelson and David Pedrick, raced under the flag of the San Diego Yacht Club.

This was the first *America*'s Cup racing series that Steven had witnessed, and he has enduring memories of the electric atmosphere in Fremantle. The hospitality that the Australians extended to him was unforgettable. The result of this very positive experience was a series of very exciting paintings.

Classic Yachts

'The Wind Piped Loudly from the West'

The Prince of Wales's (later King Edward VII) beautiful new yacht *Britannia* was launched in 1893. It promised to be an exciting racing season with the newly launched American yacht *Navahoe*, designed by Herreshoff, sailing across the Atlantic to join the 'Big Class' regatta circuit. Strong winds were forecast for the later part of August 1893 and after racing at Cowes and then Weymouth, only four of the 'Big Class' fleet headed for Torquay.

Britannia, *Navahoe* and *Calluna* started the race with their topmasts housed, but *Satanita* hauled hers up and crowded on extra sail. *Satanita* was also over the line when the starting gun fired and had to return, allowing her opponents a three-minute lead. As 'the wind piped loudly from the west' *Satanita* found the extra sail laid her over, producing too much leeway. After losing a man overboard but quickly recovering him, she eventually reduced sail and rehoused her topmast. *Navahoe* did not fare any better as she damaged her mainsail, allowing *Satanita* to overhaul her. Not prepared to risk blowing out the sail, *Navahoe* reluctantly retired. *Britannia* maintained her lead and eventually won, followed by *Calluna* and *Satanita*.

The words in the title of this painting, 'The Wind Piped Loudly from the West', were in fact also the inspiration. The line, slightly modified, came from volume II of a book first published in 1894, *Yachting* by R.T. Pritchett, The Marques of Dufferin and Ava. The book gives a very detailed description of this particular race and highlights the importance of painstaking research in Steven's paintings.

mark boats?

'An Opportune Breeze from the South-east'

This painting forms a natural pair with the previous painting. It features the same yachts during the same regatta but two days later. As can be seen there is a marked contrast in the weather between these two race days. During August of that year the West Country Regattas started off very windy, but when the big cutters arrived at Dartmouth to race in the Start Bay Yacht Club's Regatta, the wind died down. *Britannia, Navahoe, Satanita* and *Calluna* waited on the start line all morning. Eventually a gentle breeze came in from the south-east, giving the big cutters an opportunity to make a race of it. *Navahoe* crossed the line first,

followed by *Britannia* and *Calluna*, with *Satanita* bringing up the rear, having drifted onto the outer flag boat and been told to 'go on' by the committee. The breeze freshened during the race, only to die down again towards the end. *Britannia* finally won the race.

As Steven sailed his yacht out of Dartmouth one soft summer morning the weather conditions evoked a phrase he had recently read in a race description; 'an opportune breeze from the south-east'. The idea for a painting was born!

14 Sept. 1893 'Navahoe' i Britannia
B3 Brenton Reef Cup. Sketch two.

The Brenton Reef Challenge Cup – 1893

This was an American trophy and therefore raced under American Racing Rules, where the time that the leading yacht crossed the start ahead of the other was deducted at the finish to give the 'elapsed time'. The Prince of Wales's new yacht *Britannia* and the closely matched new American yacht *Navahoe* came together for the race. *Britannia* was defending the trophy that had been won by the British yacht *Genesta* in 1885.

At noon on 14 September both yachts started from the Needles for the 120-mile race to Cherbourg, round the breakwater and back. The strong easterly wind gave both yachts a 'broad reach' there and back. *Britannia* was first away after the gun, with *Navahoe* almost a minute behind. After the sixty-mile dash to Cherbourg *Navahoe* was twenty-five seconds in front, but after a short tacking battle along the two miles on the inside of the breakwater, *Britannia* had clawed back a two-and-a-half-minute lead over the American yacht.

The yachts finished the race back at the Needles in the dark, with *Britannia* leading by just fifty-seven seconds, but only two and a half seconds on 'corrected' time. However, the *Navahoe* team protested as they claimed the finish mark boat had moved and they had, as a consequence, sailed a longer course than *Britannia*. After a lengthy meeting the Royal Yacht Squadron agreed and awarded *Navahoe* the Cup.

Britannia racing *Valkyrie III* and *Ailsa* for the Muir Memorial Challenge Cup

The summer of 1895 saw the 'Big Class' fleet in the Clyde for the Scottish season. This was to be the debut for Lord Dunraven's newly completed *America*'s Cup challenger, *Valkyrie III*. She had been commissioned to replace *Valkyrie II*, which sank as the result of an unfortunate accident with *Satanita* during the Muir Memorial Challenge Cup the previous year.

Valkyrie III was extremely light with a massive sail area giving her a boom length of 105 feet, 15 feet longer than *Britannia*'s boom. This made her a fine 'light airs' yacht and indeed she beat *Britannia* in such conditions during the Clyde series. However, the Muir Memorial Challenge Cup race was held on 3 July in weather conditions better suited to *Britannia*. A gusty north-westerly proved little challenge to the royal cutter but *Valkyrie III*, with a waterline length a mere foot longer than *Britannia*'s, but carrying 3,500 square feet more canvas, found the conditions difficult. She could not carry the vast sail area in the gusty weather and spent the weather legs over on her 'beam ends'. Even so this race was to be one of the fastest matches sailed on the Clyde during those years, with *Britannia* averaging a speed of 11½ knots over the course. The final result gave *Britannia* the Cup with *Ailsa* coming home in second place.

Balloon S/sails +
spinaker.

Atlantic

This painting depicts the black-hulled schooner *Atlantic* passing Wolf Rock lighthouse as she closes on the finish of her record-breaking race across the Atlantic in 1905. The record time of twelve days, four hours, one minute and nineteen seconds still stands today. Many yachts over the years have tried to better *Atlantic*'s time. Lightweight racing machines such as Eric Tabarly's hydrofoil trimaran, and more recently *Nicorette*, have beaten the record but they have done so by choosing a weather window and racing alone. *Atlantic*'s time would have been even better if the strong winds that were with her during the crossing had not deserted her in the final few miles to the finish.

Kaiser Wilhelm II reinstated this transatlantic race in 1905 after his yacht *Meteor* had been thoroughly beaten, on many occasions, by his uncle King Edward VII's yacht *Britannia*. By sponsoring this race he hoped to improve his reputation in international yachting circles. The Ocean Cup, which the Kaiser presented, was for yachts of eighty tons or above (net Custom House Measurement), and was to be sailed without handicap or sail restriction.

Atlantic was joined on a foggy start line by two square-rigged barques, one yawl and seven schooners. At her helm was the legendary Charlie Barr of *America*'s Cup fame. During a mid-ocean storm, *Atlantic*'s owner, Wilson Marshall, came up onto the deck and asked Barr to shorten sail. Barr refused, shouting 'You hired me to win this race, and, by God, that is what I am going to do', and ordered the owner below!

Brynhild II racing off Cowes

*B*rynhild II was built by Camper and Nicholson at Gosport in 1907 for Sir James Pender. Together with *White Heather*, she was the first of the new class of 23-metre cutters designed under the International Yacht Racing Union Rules of 1906. The idea was to encourage a class of yacht that combined speed with accommodation to produce the 'cruiser racers' of the day. They were fast but wet yachts raced with a crew of twenty-two.

Brynhild II was plagued by bad luck in her first few years, from 1907 to 1910. A shipyard worker was killed by her cradle during launch; then, in her first race, one of her crew was killed when he fell from aloft, and a crewman went over the side in the Solent and drowned. Disaster struck during the Orwell Corinthian Yacht Club Regatta off Harwich in 1910. Her mast failed and drove through her hull, taking her to the bottom. *Brynhild II* was raised, and although very badly damaged, was patched up and towed to Brightlingsea, where it is assumed she underwent restoration.

In 1912 *Brynhild II* was purchased by J.F. Swann, who also owned the 150-ton ketch *Medora*, the sister ship to *Adela*. Swann cruised and raced *Brynhild II* extensively until he sold her in 1922. Coincidentally, J.F. Swann was the grandfather of Steven's great friend, the London art dealer, Oliver Swann.

Susanne racing *Westward* off the Needles

The 323-ton *Westward* was built by Nat Herreshoff on Rhode Island in 1910 for Alexander Cochran. She was commanded by one of the most famous racing skippers of all time, Captain Charlie Barr. With a hand-picked crew of thirty-one men she crossed the Atlantic for her racing debut in Kiel, Germany. As the season progressed she joined the 'Big Class' fleet in the Solent.

At this time the British handicap system for yacht racing had become so complex that the sport was in some disarray. It was into this atmosphere that *Westward* sailed in the summer of 1910. There was trouble immediately. Cochran politely but firmly refused to discuss the handicapping of his vessel with the committee. He was only willing to race her in Class A of the International Rules. As she had been built to these rules Cochran felt that *Westward* would not have a fair chance of winning in British waters if she was to be re-measured under the British rules. He went so far as to threaten to sail straight back to America if his wishes were not complied with. Eventually the committee succumbed and *Westward* raced in the Solent with great success, gaining eleven firsts out of eleven starts.

This painting depicts the great American schooner *Westward* racing against the much smaller Fife schooner *Susanne* in a brisk south-easterly breeze off the Needles. *Susanne* was given a generous time allowance in order to enable her to compete fairly against *Westward*.

Germania racing *Meteor IV*

Steven drew his inspiration for this lively painting from the effect that the narrow entrance into the Solent between Fort Albert and Hurst Castle, known as the Hurst Narrows, has on the tidal flow. The painting depicts these two magnificent schooners sailing out through Hurst Narrows on an ebb tide in a strong westerly breeze. The result is a confused sea with plenty of 'white water'.

Germania was designed by Max Oertz and built by Krupps in Germany in 1903. She visited the Solent on many occasions and raced regularly against many of the other great yachts of the time, such as *Cetonia, Susanne, Adela* and *Cicely. Meteor* was one of the largest schooners built during the early part of the last century. She was built for Kaiser Wilhelm II by the same German designer and builder as *Germania*, and was launched in 1909. She proved a very fast yacht and was only outclassed by the American schooner *Westward*.

Britannia racing off Cowes

*I*n this painting Steven recreated the weather conditions in the eastern Solent. A stiff breeze over a flood tide creates a short choppy sea, and generally when the wind is in the south-east the light is quite soft. As always, he has succeeded in recreating the atmosphere. *Britannia* excelled in these weather conditions and in this painting she is seen taking full advantage of the fast-moving flood tide, while other yachts in the race choose to keep to the calmer inshore waters on their course to the next mark.

According to Steven the composition of this painting is critical. Placing yachts in the distance and foreground helps to create depth, while the positioning of breaking waves directs the eye through the painting to the distant yachts. Even though the clouds are soft cumulus they too are placed to lead the eye through the painting from foreground to background. This painting was one of Steven's early yachting compositions and was painted at a time when he was developing several ideas and techniques that he now uses as a basic structure in all his works.

Lulworth off Old Harry Rocks, Dorset

*T*his is a beautiful yacht with a sad story. She is still in existence, although only just, stripped of everything and lying exposed to the elements in a Mediterranean shipyard. She was the subject of a protracted and bitter legal battle, the true loser of which was the yacht herself. She waits for a person with great vision and deep pockets to rescue her.

Built in 1920 for R.H. Lee by Messrs White Bros in Southampton, she was launched as *Terpsichore*. She was designed to race with the 'Big Class' but unfortunately she made an indifferent showing in her first few seasons. Lee was disappointed with her performance so in 1924 he sold her to Herbert Weld Blundell of Lulworth Castle in Dorset. Weld changed her name to *Lulworth*, and by the 1925 racing season she really started to shine. In 1926 she again changed hands and became the property of Sir Mortimer Singer, of Singer Sewing Machine fame. He raced her with great success for two seasons before she changed hands yet again in 1928, being sold to Alexander Paton.

During the 1930 season *Lulworth* was involved in a tragic accident with the 12-metre *Lucilla*. *Lulworth* ran into *Lucilla* before the start at Cowes. The 12-metre was holed and sank immediately, with the loss of one crewman. The steward had been struck on the head at the moment of impact and knocked overboard. He drowned before the rescue boat could pick him out of the water. An inquest was ordered, and although *Lulworth* raced successfully through to the end of the season, events were tainted by the tragedy.

This was to be *Lulworth*'s last racing season. It was felt that the accident with *Lucilla* was a major contributing factor in Paton's decision to retire the yacht at the end of 1930, and *Lulworth* once again found herself up for sale.

Britannia's Weather

*T*he King's yacht was famous for excelling in strong breezes from her launch in 1897 right to the end of her phenomenally long and distinguished racing career, which spanned four decades. Even well reefed and against much more modern yacht designs, she took some beating right through to the end of her life.

In order to keep *Britannia* competitive her rig was altered seven times over the years, from the original gaff rig to the final Bermuda rig. In 1925 the Scottish designer Fife was invited to design the improvements to her rig for the 1926 season when she was to be pitched against yachts such as *Lulworth*, *Westward* and *White Heather II*. Fife's improvements entailed socketing the topmast into the lower mast, replacing the more traditional overlapping fidded topmast. This saved on weight and windage, at the same time extending the height of the rig. However, the design only marginally improved *Britannia*'s performance and was changed again the following year.

Britannia is Steven's all-time favourite yacht. From every angle her lines are perfect, making her a joy to paint. Her black hull made her instantly recognisable, even from a distance, and the colour of her hull contrasted beautifully with her cream cotton sails.

B12 Beat to the Needles

Beat to the Needles

This race around the Isle of Wight took place as part of the Royal Thames and Royal Victoria Yacht Club joint regatta in the late summer of 1926. The race was for vessels of more than TM tons 110 and the line-up for the day consisted of *Lulworth, Britannia, White Heather II, Westward* and *Susanne*. The start line was off Ryde on a perfect summer's day with a good breeze. All the yachts sailed on a level handicap except the smaller yacht *Susanne*, which was given a forty-five-minute head start for the race.

It was a most exciting event; the yachts raced within yards of each other around the island. In this large painting Steven has depicted the beat from St Catherine's Point to the Needles mark.

At this stage *Lulworth* had just sailed through the fleet to take the lead, closely followed by *Britannia* and then *White Heather II*. *Susanne* is in the foreground with *Westward* to weather of her. It was to be a fight to the finish. *Westward* gained the lead from *Lulworth* as they hoisted spinnakers for the run down the Solent, but *Lulworth* fought back and stole first prize from *Westward* only a few hundred yards from the line. *Lulworth* won by a tiny margin of only two seconds, quite an amazing result when one considers that they had raced over a course of fifty-four nautical miles! It must have been a thrilling sight to see these magnificent yachts battling at such close quarters on a sparkling day.

Lulworth and *Shamrock* off the Needles

By 1929 *Lulworth*'s racing career was reaching its zenith. She won the season quite decisively, being five points ahead of the mighty American schooner *Westward* and seven points ahead of both *White Heather II* and *Shamrock*. This painting illustrates beautifully *Lulworth*'s racing prowess during the summer of 1929.

The Royal Victoria Yacht Club Regatta opened with a race around the Isle of Wight for the 'Big Class' yachts. The day started very slowly with little wind as the fleet worked its way down the Solent in an easterly direction from the start line at Ryde. As the yachts rounded the eastern tip of the island the wind freshened, and by the time *Lulworth* and *Shamrock* reached the Needles they were locked in a battle for the lead. Once they rounded the Needles light and moved into the calmer waters, however, *Lulworth*'s superiority came to the fore and she went on to take first prize by a margin of only forty-one seconds after an eight-hour race.

Steven commented that 'the cliffs above Scratchells Bay on the south coast of the Isle of Wight make a perfect backdrop for a painting such as this, highlighting the drama of the battle between these two giant yachts.'

Storming through Cowes Roads

One of the most exhilarating experiences for a yachtsman when sailing in the Solent is to have plenty of wind and very little sea. In this painting we see *Westward, Britannia, Astra* and *Shamrock* with reefed mainsails, heeling under the pressure of a breezy south-westerly. These hard-driven yachts would have been an awesome sight as they beat past the Yacht Squadron and headed down the Solent to the next race mark.

The 'Big Class' fleet arrived on the south coast from the Harwich regatta, and for the first time in the 1931 season *Shamrock* was to be given some serious competition. *Britannia* had been modified to race under the new 'J' Class rule, and sporting a Bermuda rig she worked her way through the fleet to end the season second on points, while *Shamrock* held onto the lead.

Britannia had always done very well in a hard breeze, whereas her results in light airs had been disappointing. However, with her new rig she seemed to have gained a distinct advantage in light winds – weather conditions that had been, thus far, dominated by *Shamrock.*

Solent Fortnight – 1932

By 1932 the era of the 'Big Class' yachts was drawing to a close as the American 'J' Class rule was beginning to be introduced. The yachts started the season racing under a wide range of rating rules, producing dispirited racing and predictable results. Then to everyone's surprise *Astra* took the radical step of reducing her canvas by some 200 feet, therefore reducing her rating and bringing her into line with the American rules. *Candida* then *Britannia* quickly followed this action. By Cowes Week of that year these three yachts were sailing on even terms. The season was beginning to look more challenging. The reduction in sail area had not affected the yachts' boat speed against the rest of the fleet but substantially increased their time allowances. The result of this was that soon after Cowes Week both *White Heather* and *Shamrock V* took action and reduced their sail areas. By the end of the season the whole of the 'Big Class' were sailing on even terms. Even at her grand old age *Britannia* was still sparkling and won the season beating, the 'J' Class *Shamrock V* by three points.

Against Wind and Tide

As any skipper of a yacht soon discovers, when sailing against the tide there is always an advantage to be had from staying in shallow waters, as tidal speed is less than in the deeper part of a channel. This is particularly so when sailing and racing in the Solent. Here, the 'Big Class' yachts are racing westwards 'against wind and tide' and are short tacking up the north shore of the Solent. Steven has rarely painted the 'Big Class' with the north shore in the background as, unlike the Isle of Wight, the mainland shore is fairly flat and featureless.

As the yachts are being viewed from the south-west the sun is shining onto their sails, as opposed to through them, as is the case in many of Steven's paintings, where the sails are backlit by the sun. Steven has used a Turneresque technique of painting light areas against dark areas to help create an illusion of depth. He has also angled the yachts so that the sun 'spotlights' the animated crew activity.

Laying the Mark

During 1935 the American 'J' Class yacht *Yankee* sailed over from America to join in the British racing circuit. This, as usual, started at Harwich and moved round the coast during the summer, taking in other yacht racing centres such as Southend, Cowes, Torquay and Dartmouth. It took some time for the visitors to become acquainted with the unfamiliar British racing rules as well as the strong tides and unpredictable weather. This was particularly apparent when racing off Cowes.

In 'Laying the Mark' *Yankee* is preparing her spinnaker pole and hauling out on deck her spinnaker as she approaches the next mark, but as she is on port tack she has to sail below *Shamrock* which is on starboard tack, giving *Shamrock* right of way. *Shamrock* has her pole set up on the mast and is already hoisting her spinnaker as she rounds the mark. Ahead of her with their spinnakers already set and pulling hard are *Candida*, *Velsheda* and *Endeavour*.

The idea for this painting came whilst Steven was viewing some archive footage of one of the 'J' Class boats hoisting a spinnaker. He was astonished at how quickly the crew managed to get the spinnaker up. Steven wanted to paint a picture that illustrated the sequence of yachts coming up to the mark, rounding, hoisting the spinnakers and sailing away.

Squadron Start

*I*n 1935, after twenty-five years of competitive racing, the 323-ton schooner *Westward* was losing her supremacy to the new 'J' Class yachts. The forty-two-year-old cutter *Britannia*, although rigged to compete against the 'J's, could no longer keep pace with the likes of *Velsheda*.

This was to be the last racing season for both *Westward* and *Britannia*. Sadly, on 20 January 1936 King George V died suddenly. In compliance with the King's wishes, *Britannia* was scuttled in St Catherine's Deep, to the south of the Isle of Wight. As a mark of respect and for the affection he held for the King, T.B. Davis ceased to race his magnificent schooner, *Westward*. She spent the rest of her life cruising around the coasts of Europe.

Double Reef Racing

*T*he two following paintings are studies of the same moment in a race but painted from two different viewpoints.

After racing in comparatively light airs during the West Country Regatta, the final two days of the 1935 season at Dartmouth provided the 'Big Class' fleet with some real heavy weather. On 30 August a strong south-westerly forced the abandonment of the first day's racing, although *Yankee* was keen to race. Her competitors were reluctant to race, but eventually joined her out in Start Bay. The big 'J' Class boats, double reefed and punching up and down the start line in a sizeable swell, were soon joined by the committee boat, only to be told that the race officers had decided the rough conditions were too dangerous and had cancelled the race. The second day was not much better, but the race committee did allow the racing to go ahead. However, two of the fleet, *Astra* and *Candida*, stayed in port, believing the conditions were still too bad.

Shamrock is shown on port tack dipping behind *Endeavour* as *Yankee* makes a very good start, going over the line at ten knots only two seconds after the gun, closely followed by *Velsheda* to leeward. Just after gybing around the first mark a fierce squall hit *Yankee*, with dire consequences. Her mast crumpled and crashed to the deck. Two of her crew were flung over the side but were quickly recovered. The race was abandoned immediately by the other yachts and the accident ended *Yankee*'s racing for that season.

Dainty

On Steven's first visit to Bermuda he was introduced to the owner of a yacht that was housed in the Bermuda Maritime Museum. *Dainty* is a lovely-looking yacht, but what was is it about her that warranted 'museum status'? Her story started in 1897. She was built on a Bermudan beach for a British Army officer who rejected her immediately because she had been built with a spoon bow instead of the swan bow he had requested. However, with her pretty shape and strong construction, *Dainty* charmed a succession of owners. She was raced both locally and on long-distance ocean races. Often on the ocean races she was Bermuda's only entrant! *Dainty*'s robust construction saw her through two groundings during hurricanes in 1931 and 1987.

Because of *Dainty*'s age and long association with Bermuda, her last owners, Michael and Terri Drew, had planned, eventually, to donate her to the museum. Unfortunately the last storm damaged her very badly and the decision was made to donate her sooner rather than later, or risk losing her altogether in any subsequent storms. The affection for the yacht in Bermuda is so great that money, equipment and help poured into the restoration project even before it was announced that she was to be permanently displayed at the museum.

This painting depicts *Dainty* leaving Bermuda in 1923 to join the Bermuda Ocean Race, which was the forerunner to the Newport to Bermuda Race. *Dainty* finished second behind the American yacht *Memory*. She was the first Bermudan yacht home, which gave the islanders cause for great celebration.

Mariette – The Atlantic Challenge, 1997

In 1997 the New York Yacht Club, the Royal Cornwall Yacht Club and the Royal Yacht Squadron organised the re-enactment of the famous 1905 Ocean Cup race. They invited heavy-displacement super yachts from around the world to take part. The race committee strove to keep the format of the race as close to the original as possible. The same start line was laid as in 1905 but with a tug marking the windward end of the line, replacing the now long gone *Sand Hook Light Vessel.*

The schooner *Atlantic* won the 1905 race, completing the crossing between Sandy Hook and the Lizard in Cornwall in twelve days, four hours and one minute – a record she still holds today for an Atlantic crossing under racing conditions.

Mr T. Perkins, the owner of the 1915 schooner, *Mariette*, commissioned Steven to record his graceful yacht's participation in this great race. Steven and Oliver Swann travelled to New York together to witness the start. It was Steven's first trip to New York, and during his stay he was given the opportunity to visit the famous Trophy Room in the New York Yacht Club's headquarters on West Forty-fourth Street. Here he was able to spend some valuable time studying the remarkable collection of models of *America*'s Cup yachts.

Race day dawned grey and overcast, affording only glimpses of the sun. In order to give Steven a good vantage point from which to make sketches and take photographs of the start Oliver managed to secure places for them aboard the tug which marked the end of the line. However, the wind direction called for a reaching start and all the yachts heeled away from them, showing more antifoul than deck detail! Steven commented, 'this was visually uninspiring for the painting I had in mind but I had videoed and photographed the pre-start manoeuvres so I had plenty of reference material. I made sketches, imagining the view from the other end of the line back towards the tug I was observing the race from.'

Unfortunately, the wind for the Atlantic crossing was unreliable, and time constraints meant that many of the yachts had to motor sail for periods of time to enable them to complete the voyage. Therefore, the record still stands, tantalising, for another year.

Velsheda sail trials.

Velsheda – Sail Trials in the Solent

After a distinguished racing career in the 1930s, *Velsheda* languished for many years on a mud berth in the Hamble. Eventually restored on a tight budget in 1983, and with her original racing rig, she spent several years sailing in the Solent. At that time *Velsheda* had no auxiliary power, and the old skills of sailing a magnificent yacht of this kind had to be relearned.

Velsheda then passed into the ownership of a gentleman who had the desire to restore her but not the required resources. She again sat on her mud berth, but by this time she was in a truly sorry state. Stripped of all her fittings and fixtures and open to the weather she was indeed a pitiful sight, which is how she looked when the present owner first saw her one raw February morning. Two years later in September 1997, she emerged from Southampton Yacht Services yard the sleek and gleaming beauty that she is today.

On this day in September as *Velsheda* made her swift passage up the Solent showing off her new suit of sails, Steven was sitting in the yacht club in Yarmouth enjoying a beer with friends. When *Velsheda* came into view he leapt to his feet, made a hasty exit and raced to get his camera and RIB and give chase! This painting was the result of that afternoon.

Moonbeam – The Fife Regatta, 1998

The Scottish artist Alastair Housen organised the first Fife Regatta. He invited Fife-built yachts from all over the world to the Clyde, Scotland, during the early summer of 1998.

Steven and Oliver Swann drove up to Scotland trailing Steven's RIB. Oliver had volunteered to drive the RIB for Steven while he took photographs. As they drove north through the night the weather deteriorated, which wasn't going to make for very exciting paintings. Steven said, 'No one wants to hang gloom on the wall. No yachtsman wants to be reminded about the down side of sailing, least of all me!'

They launched the RIB in the morning gloom and found the fleet gilling around in the drizzle waiting for the start. This was the penultimate day of the regatta and the weather remained the same throughout the race, so other than at the start, it was difficult to make out the yachts' relevant positions through the mist! The following day was, thankfully, clearer and brighter, revealing the true grandeur of the Scottish scenery. The race started at the Kyles of Bute. There was little wind but the light was excellent. Oliver carefully positioned the RIB so that Steven could get the photographs he wanted of the backlit effect of the sun on the sails. He had the idea for a painting that would 'show off' *Moonbeam*'s beautiful cream-coloured sails.

Kentra – The Fife Regatta, 1998

*K*entra and *Moonbeam* had both made the long journey from the Mediterranean to take part in this regatta, and here they are captured on canvas, tacking majestically against the light westerly breeze, a spectacular sight against the beautiful backdrop of the Scottish scenery. These graceful yachts exemplify William Fife's mastery of design, and it was a feast for the eyes to have so many of his yachts together again at their birthplace on the Clyde. During the regatta Steven made careful studies of all the participating yachts, in particular deck and crew details. The inspiration for this painting of *Kentra* and *Moonbeam* came in an instant, when the sun flashed off *Moonbeam*'s varnished boom.

A sad point, worthy of note, was that the famous yachtsman, Eric Tabarly, fell from his beautiful yacht *Pen Duick IV* and drowned, as he sailed her up the west coast of Britain to take part in the regatta. It is a sobering reminder to all of us that even for a sailor with Eric's wealth of experience the sea can be unforgiving.

Velsheda wins the Start

Antigua Classic Week 1999 was the scene of an historic event. Three 'J' Class yachts were on the start line, together for the first time since the 1930s. The three surviving yachts *Shamrock V* (1930), *Velsheda* (1933) and *Endeavour* (1934), came together to challenge for the *Velsheda* Trophy. The regatta is held in April each year and in 1999 the weather conditions could not have suited the 'big boats' better! An average breeze of twenty-five knots from the north gave the crews of these mighty yachts a challenging three days of racing. The overall winner on handicap was *Shamrock V* with *Velsheda* the fastest of the three yachts over the water, taking line honours for each race.

This was a particularly important regatta for Steven. It was his first time in the Caribbean and, although he has been painting the 'J' Class yachts for years and had seen them all individually, sailing in different parts of the world, he had never actually witnessed them racing. From a painter's point of view the Caribbean presented its own set of challenges; Steven had to create a totally new colour palette in order to recreate the intensity of light and colour. This picture was the first of three outstanding paintings Steven was inspired to create from this Caribbean experience.

Modern Yachts

maiden

Maiden in the Southern Ocean

It took a great deal of courage for Tracey Edwards to realise her ambition to sail a yacht around the world with an all-female crew, in one of the toughest races on earth, the Whitbread Round the World Race. Against all odds, using strength of personality and tenacity, she put together a formidable team of women and persuaded Royal Jordanian Airlines to sponsor her. *Maiden* completed the gruelling, nine-month race, coming second in class but winning the hearts of the nation.

In this painting Steven has captured the exhilaration that the *Maiden* crew experienced when surfing, on the very edge of control, down the backs of the towering waves that travel unimpeded around the globe, in the Southern Ocean. Steven's experience as a yachtsman, although on a totally different scale, gave him a clue to the sensation the girls must have experienced in those brief moments when a wave picks up the boat and it surges forwards and downwards at great speed.

"Jazz Sensation" (this boat was "off station" but was in this position)   committee boats   "Taipan of Wales" RTYC (Crew giving salute)   "Carronade"   "Akela"   "Whitecap"   Harbour Court   Flag pole   "Belvedere" (at anchor)

New York Yacht Club Sesquicentennial Regatta

Being commissioned by the New York Yacht Club to paint a picture to mark the 150th anniversary of the club was a great honour for Steven. While he was gathering information for this commission the Yacht Club extended every hospitality to Steven, making the visit one of the highlights of his painting career.

The painting itself proved quite complex, and as usual the use of stills and video cameras was invaluable. Steven used the still shots for yacht and background detail and the video for sequential placing of the various line astern yachts. No 'artist's licence' is used here! However, as this was a sailing yacht regatta

Steven did manage to include some yachts actually sailing to contrast against the 'bare pole' procession and to help create the feel of a breeze for the upcoming racing.

The harbour start procession had in the Yacht Club's customary fashion been meticulously planned, all except for the weather. The first few mornings dawned to the notorious Rhode Island fog, and the procession Steven had hoped to paint was repeatedly cancelled. He waited nervously as the days ticked by. No photographs, no painting! Finally the penultimate day of the regatta dawned clear and Steven was able to get his pictures.

Sigma 38s racing off Ryde

The down side of yachting in Northern European waters – the grey drizzling dawns, the rolling listless swells, the 'graveyard' watches, wet oilskins – are all forgotten on those all too rare occasions when the sailing conditions are perfect. A fifteen to twenty knot breeze, a lively sea and leading the fleet in a race make it worthwhile. On such a day, whilst on a short passage from Yarmouth to Portsmouth, aboard his yacht *Fine Art*, Steven passed a large fleet of Sigma 38s. At the head of the fleet was the distinctive green hull of *Yeoman XXVIII* owned by David Aisher. She rounded the mark, off Ryde, and having dropped her spinnaker, beat back west.

As always, Steven had his camera to hand and took numerous photographic notes, focusing on the crew activity as they wrestled with the headsails and straining spinnakers. This was 'round the cans' sailing at its best. The excellent design of the Sigma 38s lends itself to this type of sailing as the well balanced fractional rig makes these yachts easy to handle with an amateur crew.

The ideas for this painting came easily as even the scudding clouds added to the drama by casting shadows over the water and yachts. Steven often uses the effect of light and shadow in his paintings to create a feeling of depth. As the final Sigma rounded the mark Steve continued on his way towards Portsmouth buzzing with inspiration.

C4 Rolex Swan Regatta.

Rolex Swan Regatta

The winds for the 1997 Swan Rolex Regatta, Cowes, Isle of Wight, were light, so the race organisers kept the race courses short, which provided plenty of close and exciting action for the owners and crews. This particular race day dawned quietly, with the start being delayed due to lack of wind. However, the westerly wind came up and freshened quickly to produce sparkling racing on a boisterous sea in bright sunshine.

This painting was commissioned by the owner of the well-known Swan 46 II *Crackerjack*. Steven's brief was to paint *Crackerjack* while she was racing, which would seem simple enough. However, painting modern yachts racing, with their large headsails, presents its own set of problems. Showing a yacht off at its best, with plenty of deck detail and crew action, means viewing it from the stern quarter. The trouble is that *Crackerjack* is racing, and to show this, must be set in context with other yachts in the background. These yachts would therefore be to windward and in front of the main subject! The only solution to this dilemma was to paint the yacht catching up with the class in front. *Crackerjack* was in Class II and fortunately the owner/skipper is a very successful helmsman, and at this point in the race *Crackerjack* genuinely did catch up with the back of the Class I fleet, making Steven's job easier.

Steven looks at the Swans, not purely from an artist's point of view, but also with an owner's eye. He regularly sailed his own Swan 44 *Fine Art* around the south coast of England and competed in the Swan Rolex Regatta in Cowes in 1999.

6 Metres rounding the Leeward Mark

Although the 6 Metre yacht did not have a big following in the UK, the 6 Metre class world-wide has maintained a healthy presence, mainly in Sweden and Finland. A recent survey found that out of 144 post-1920-registered 6 Metres, 123 could be accounted for and that all those still in existence are either sailing or undergoing restoration.

During the 1930s 6 Metre class racing was in its heyday. This well-proportioned classic yacht with long graceful overhangs visually complemented the elements of wind and water. *Sea Venture* (K2) is about to lower her spinnaker as she approaches the leeward mark, hard on the heels of *Lucia* (US55), owned by Briggs S. Cunningham. She has already hardened up on starboard tack for the lively beat to the next mark.

Etchells in Great Sound

*I*n 1965 the search was on for a new Olympic keelboat class. The American boat builder and designer Skip Etchells came up with a design, and although the Soling was eventually picked as the new Olympic boat, the Etchells went on to become one of the most popular keelboats of modern times, with fifty active fleets world-wide.

There is a large fleet of these fast and exhilarating boats in Bermuda. During Bermuda International Race Week, held each spring, Etchells skippers from all over the world fly there to compete. Whilst Etchells do not have the classic lines of the International One Design, they are very efficient racing machines, able to tack through seventy degrees, and are fast, stable and simple to sail for a three-man crew.

Bermuda 'Fitted Dinghy' Racing

The 'Fitted Dinghy' is unique to Bermuda in size and sail area. They are very strongly built to carry a large crew. The uniqueness of these vessels is only matched by the rather unorthodox racing rules. The crew are allowed to jump overboard if there is a need to lighten the load should the wind drop, and the racing rules allow the boats to finish with only one person aboard. The style of the crewmen's exit is usually flamboyant and crowd pleasing, but the extra push to the transom as they depart can give the boat enough extra momentum to win the race!

The racing rules state that, unlike the more usual port gives way to starboard rule, the boats must tack away when converging. These boats are very difficult to tack because of their large sail area, which makes for exciting entertainment for the spectators. When it is breezy all the crew sit on the weather gunwale to counterbalance the boat, except for one crewman whose job it is to continually bail because of the low freeboard. Match racing of these dinghies between two rival Bermudan Dinghy Clubs goes back many years and the cup most keenly fought over is the 'Jubilee Cup'.

Gordie Walker, who owns, amongst many, the Fitted Dinghy *Victory*, put Steven in the right place on the various race-courses aboard his motor yacht *Onion Patch*. Steven witnessed at close hand some of the racing that inspired the paintings of yachts racing in Bermuda.

J. Steven Dews

IODs close tacking in Great Sound

One of the few places in the world where there is a large fleet of International One Design (IOD) yachts is Bermuda. These GRP yachts have classic lines reminiscent of the old 6 Metre yachts. One Design racing always provides exciting sport because the yachts, sails and crew skills are closely matched. After the start the fleet spreads out on different tacks as individual boat tactics come into play. The real fun begins at the first mark when all the boats converge, making for tense, close manoeuvring. A favoured wind shift can easily put a trailing boat in the lead!

Top-class yachtsmen from all over the world come together in Bermuda each year to take part in the fleet racing and match racing tournaments. The crews swap boats every day throughout the regatta. Although the boats are similar each will have its own idiosyncrasies. This form of racing results in yachtsmen winning purely on their helming, tactical and crewing skills. One of the oldest IOD match racing regattas is sailed annually in Bermuda. The King Edward VII Gold Cup, dating back to 1937, is recognised as one of the foremost match racing events in the world.

Sailing Ships

The Battle of Copenhagen, 2 April 1801

At 9.45 a.m. on 2 April 1801 the signal was made for Nelson's fleet to weigh anchor and make their way to the Channel and put themselves into position, planned the night before, opposite the Danish defences. *Edgar* had been chosen to head the line. She sailed round the lugger that was marking the southern tip of the middle ground shoal and stood down the channel, holding her fire until she was in position. *Ardent*, some distance astern, ran down and placed herself just ahead of *Edgar*. Elsewhere, however, things were not going according to plan. *Agamemnon*, trying to beat against the wind, ran aground on the shoal before she reached the lugger. *Bellona*, after having been warned that she was 'standing into danger' and 'to engage the enemy closer' by Nelson on his flagship *Elephant*, ran aground on a spur. This was a blow to Nelson as the Danes already outnumbered him. He then had to place his ship where *Bellona* was to fight. To add to his problems *Russell*, in the now dense smoke, followed *Bellona* onto the middle grounds shoal. Even with three ships missing from the original fleet of twelve, Nelson won the day. The fact that the British gun crews were more highly trained than the Danes led to the British victory.

Wanderer off Spurn Point

Wanderer was built in 1844 as a trader for William Priest. Unfortunately, she was lost a mere nine years later in 1853.

As with the painting of *Phoenix*, illustrated elsewhere in this book, this painting of *Wanderer* was influenced by the work of the nineteenth-century Hull artist, John Ward. Steven admired Ward's eye for technical detail and enjoyed the challenge of painting Ward's vessels in a more twentieth-century form. Ward's style of sea painting, particularly rough seas, was typical of his period. Steven learnt a great deal from analysing Ward's interpretation of water. The River Humber is very opaque, with a unique colour, and John Ward had the ability to capture this perfectly. The information gained from Steve's close observation of Ward's brush strokes and colour build-up has been invaluable throughout his career.

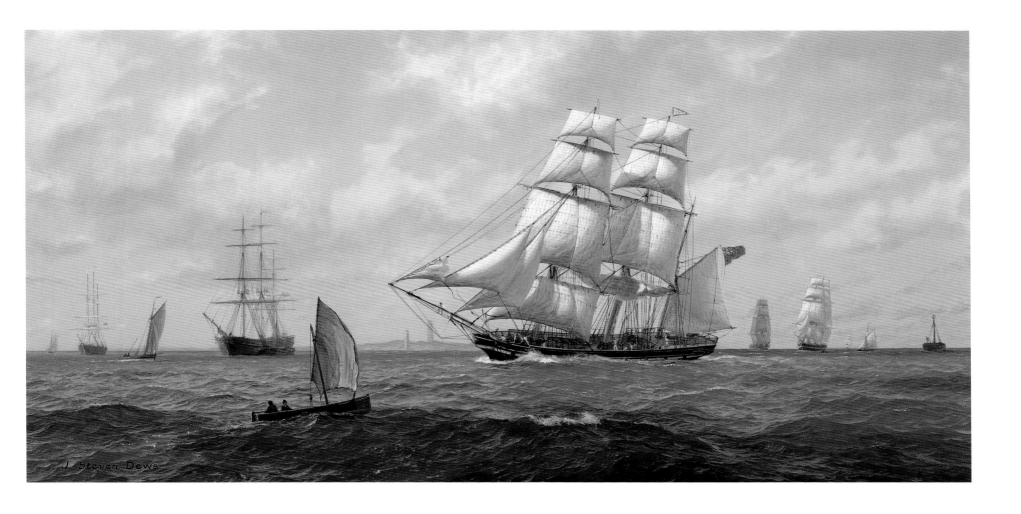

J Steven Dews

The Whaler *Phoenix,* off Greenwich – 1820

One of the most important influences on Steven's work has been the Hull marine artist John Ward, who was well known for his paintings set around the Humber Estuary in the early part of the nineteenth century. Ward died of cholera in 1849, one hundred years before Steven was born. Steven admired Ward's technical mastery and, as a young man, spent many hours in the Ferens Art Gallery in Hull, analysing Ward's techniques.

This painting is one of Steven's earliest works in which he tests some of the ideas he has gleaned from his study of Ward. This picture is the result of painstaking research. The sail plan and lines for *Phoenix* were taken from a scrimshaw whale's tooth that was exhibited at the Hull Town Docks Museum. The background in the painting depicts Greenwich exactly as it looked in 1820, and required some in-depth research, including a trip to Blackwall Reach to sketch the shape of the river and Greenwich on the opposite bank of the Thames. This proved a difficult task, as the Thames waterfront is now so built up that many walls had to be scaled in the name of art!

Tweed in the Channel

Tweed was launched as *Punjaub* in Bombay in 1854. She was originally built of the very finest Malabar teak as a paddle-wheel frigate for the Indian Navy, serving in the Persian War in 1855 and the Indian Mutiny of 1857.

In 1862 she sailed to London for a refit, but by the time she arrived there the Indian Navy had merged with the Royal Navy and *Punjaub* was offered for sale. John Willis bought her to add to his fleet. He converted her into a sailing ship at great expense and renamed her *Tweed*. She became his favourite ship and the flagship of his company. Her nickname was *Willie's Wonder* due to her exceptionally fast passage times. It was said at the time that there was no clipper ship that could better her. She possessed a fine hull shape and a lofty rig. During her merchant days she was used to lay part of the Persian Gulf cable to Bombay, as a troop carrier bringing troops back home to England from India and as a passenger ship to Australia.

In July 1988 *Tweed* was dismasted in Algoa Bay and had to be towed into Port Elizabeth for repairs. However, upon inspection she was found to be too old and leaky to be worth repairing and the decision was made to break her up. Her teak frames and planks were used to roof a church in Port Elizabeth.

Ariel Leaving London Docks – 1866

riel was a composite-built tea clipper made by Robert Steele & Co. of Greenock and launched in 1865 for Shaw, Lowther & Maxton of London. She measured 197 feet 4 inches and displaced 852.7 tons. Having the same exceptional sea-keeping qualities as her sister ship *Taeping*, *Ariel* made some outstanding passage times. In The Great Tea Race of 1866 the ships sailed from China in just ninety-nine days, with *Ariel* beating her close rival *Taeping* by only ten minutes. However, because *Taeping* got a faster tug to tow her up the Thames to the docks she managed to dock twenty minutes before *Ariel*. As the race was so close the ships' owners split the extra bonus of ten shillings per ton awarded for the first of the season's tea to arrive in London. On *Ariel*'s return run to Hong Kong in 1866 she broke another record. She left London Docks on 13 October, under the command of Captain Keay, and completed the voyage, from pilot to pilot, in only seventy-nine days and twenty-one hours.

In the early days of Steven's career as a marine artist he was best known for his paintings of sailing ships. As a child he spent all his leisure time making working models of ships and studying the works of H.A. Underhill. Underhill wrote highly detailed accounts of the intricacies of ship masting and rigging. Steven's early studies gave him the skill to produce paintings with unrivalled technical accuracy.

Ariel and '*Taeping* – The Great Tea Race' of 1866

*T*his painting depicts *Ariel* and *Taeping* battling up the Channel on the last furious leg as they raced to London. One can imagine the high adrenaline levels in every one of the crew members aboard those ships as they pushed the vessels to the limits as they passed Portland Bill.

These great races home from China with the season's first tea could be said to be the forerunners of today's epic ocean yacht racing. The ships were designed and built for speed; they were manned by highly skilled crews and commanded by exceptionally brave and talented captains. The ships often raced 'in company' for days on end, which increased the tension and excitement aboard the vessels. The captains took hair-raisingly dangerous short cuts through treacherous channels to save precious hours, often with dire consequences. The glory was great for the winning vessels. Not only was there the kudos for the crews of being part of the winning team, but there was a substantial monetary prize for the first ship home.

Sobraon alongside at Pitt Street, Circular Quay, Sydney – 1871

A very early sepia photograph of Circular Quay, Sydney, sparked the idea for this painting. Next, Steven had to find a suitable ship to add to the scene. Research led him to choose *Sobraon*. At 317 feet and 2,131 tons, at the time she was the largest composite-built ship. Her solid teak construction on iron frames was copper fastened. Built by Messrs Hall of Aberdeen and launched in 1866, she spent the majority of her working life carrying passengers between England and the Antipodes. A very fast and comfortable vessel, she was popular with the passengers, as was her kindly captain, J.A. Elmslie, who commanded her for twenty-four years from 1867. During her career in the Australian run she carried such notable people as Lord and Lady Belmore to take up the governorship of New South Wales, and Mr Ducane, to govern Tasmania.

Sobraon's last run from England was in 1891. After discharging her passengers in Melbourne she took on ballast for the trip round to Sydney where she was sold to the New South Wales Government, to be used as a reformatory ship. She lay on her mooring in Sydney Harbour for the next twenty years. Finally, the State Government handed her over to the Australian Government in 1911. Still in fine condition, despite her age, she was converted into a sail training ship for the Australian Navy.

St Ives

This is one of a series of Steven's early paintings of beach and harbour scenes. These paintings were predominantly set in the nineteenth century, around Devon and Cornwall, and many of the pictures depicted the wrecks of ships that had foundered around the rocky coast. This painting, however, is of a much more tranquil scene. It is low water; there is a stillness in the harbour, with children collecting shells at the water's edge, the mooring chains lying slack on the sand and people going about their business on this temporary landscape. Soon the tide will turn and the scene will be one of animation as the sea moves in under the hulls of the vessels. This type of painting gave Steven the opportunity to make more detailed studies of people and to explore man's relationship with the sea. In this scene man has control; he meets the sea on his own terms. Time is short, however, and there is an air of anticipation of the returning tide.

HMS *Challenger* off Bermuda

*T*his picture is one of three Steven painted of the steam corvette *Challenger*. He admired the lines of this ship as her straight sheer gave a strong visual image of power. In 1872 the Royal Navy loaned *Challenger* to take a group of scientists from the University of Edinburgh and the Royal Society on a journey that was to cover more than 68,000 nautical miles and take four years to complete. The expedition, which was subsidised by the government of the day, set out to explore the undersea world. They studied the ocean currents, depths, temperature, geology and biology of oceans.

Challenger was essentially a sailing ship. Although she was fitted with a 1,200-horsepower steam engine, this was only used for manoeuvring in port and whilst she was trawling the seabed. Below deck she was fitted out with the laboratories and workshops that the scientists would need for the expedition, and fifteen of her seventeen guns were removed for the voyage.

This painting depicts *Challenger* off the coast of Bermuda in 1873, dredging the sea floor for specimens of coral and other flora and fauna. At this point she is 'hove to' with her sails backed as she retrieves the trawl.

Sir Winston Churchill

As a fifteen-year-old schoolboy, with a passion for the sea and sailing, Steven remembers the excitement he felt when he heard that a local shipyard, Richard Dunstan's Haven of Hessle, had won the contract to build Britain's first purpose-built sail training ship. She was to be called *Sir Winston Churchill*, designed by Camper and Nicholson and built of steel. This three-masted schooner has a powerful rig and the graceful lines of a yacht.

Designed to be as labour intensive as possible for the forty-two officers and cadets, no winches meant all hand hauling, as this was the point of her existence, to develop team spirit. According to Steven, 'the sails stay on the deck unless the crew pull together.' Steven had firsthand experience of this as an adult when he served on her as a watch officer for two weeks. He has never forgotten the experience. Twenty years on he remembers every happy detail of that voyage. Years after his trip he was very proud to accept a commission from Richard Dunston to paint *Sir Winston Churchill*. Dunston requested that the ship be painted off Whitby, which, coincidentally is Steven's favourite Yorkshire port.

Tall Ships – Bermuda

Because of Bermuda's excellent harbour in Hamilton and the island's convenient geographical position, the island often plays host to large fleets of tall ships and sail training ships as they move around the globe. One of the most impressive gatherings was in 1976. The start line for this race, off the island's shore, was arguably quite narrow. The breeze was good, allowing the ships to spread most of their canvas. This made a spectacular sight at close hand, but two of the ships collided at the start and were extensively damaged. Both ships had to withdraw from the race, much to the disappointment of their young trainee crews. This painting of the 1976 race is just before the start, with *Juan Sebastian de Elcano* and *Libertad* converging, which resulted in the inevitable collision. *Libertad* was later disqualified.

In June 2000 the tall ships again gathered in Hamilton on their way to America. Whilst still an amazing sight, the start of the race was a disappointment. Due to very light winds, most of the sailing ships had to depart under motor.

The Bicentennial First Fleet
arriving at Botany Bay, January 1988

*I*n January 1988 Australia celebrated the bicentenary of the country's founding as a British colony. The highlight of this historic event was the re-enactment of the original voyage of the eleven ships that sailed from England to Sydney in 1788. The man with the vision to put this ambitious scheme together was Jonathan King, a direct descendant of one of the members of the first fleet. When he first mooted the idea of the re-enactment, the reaction from his fellow Australians was one of ridicule and criticism. Undaunted by the resistance he encountered, right up until the day the ships arrived in Sydney, he kept the plan on schedule. He attracted the support of Sir Edmund Hillary, Thor Heyerdahl, Alan Villiers and two successive Prime Ministers of Australia, Malcolm Fraser and Bob Hawkes, and finally, Buckingham Palace.

The Queen and Prince Philip inspected the fleet before its departure from Portsmouth on a voyage that was to cover 32,000 sea miles and take nine months to complete. Unfortunately, the journey was not without its problems and mishaps. By the time the fleet arrived in Brazil there was such a shortage of funds that the whole plan nearly ended there. Thanks to the efforts of an Australian radio station, 2GB Sydney, which launched an appeal for financial help, the fleet was able to continue its voyage. Tragedy also struck one of the ships, when a crew member was lost overboard whilst changing sails in the dark. His body was never recovered.

Steven was invited by the then Maritime Services Board of New South Wales to record the event for them on canvas. Steven was flown over Botany Bay in a seaplane as the ships arrived. He photographed the ships individually and made copious notes to help him formulate a composition that would illustrate the order of the ships, whilst giving each vessel equal significance.

Australia Day

This painting of the arrival of the ships at Sydney was a very complicated endeavour. Steven had to choose a moment that would represent the arrival of the fleet as well as capture the jubilant atmosphere of the day as the spectator boats escorted the eleven ships from the Heads to Farm Cove. Farm Cove, opposite the Opera House, is the exact spot where the original eleven ships had anchored two hundred years before.

Steven was given the use of a helicopter for the day, from which to take his photographic notes. The day before Australia Day, he had the opportunity to fly the course that the ships were to take as they paraded through the harbour. This gave him a chance to plan the various angles that would give the best views and start to work out ideas for the painting. The only difficulty was that, because of flight regulations, the helicopter was unable to fly below five hundred feet and Steven's planning for the best angles had been from fifteen feet. Luckily, he had taken the precaution of recording all the news coverage as a backup. From the aerial notes and video footage Steven chose the moment when *Soren Larsen* finally dropped anchor in Farm Cove with the rest of the fleet sailing in behind her. It was the moment when history had been made, two hundred years before.

Cape Horn

Cape Horn

*T*his painting is unique. In Steven's twenty-five-year career as a marine artist this is the only painting he has produced without a vessel of some description in it. This picture also has an intrinsic importance to Steven as it represents the essence of all his work, man's relationship with the sea. It represents a lifetime of passion and wonder.

Cape Horn is the ultimate challenge for all sailors, from the crews of the mighty clipper ships as they raced around the globe to the modern-day yachtsman as they carve through the Southern Ocean in their high-tech vessels. Steven's painting graphically illustrates the unforgiving, desolate environment, which fills the hearts of all sailors with trepidation.

This was one of the most challenging paintings that Steven has undertaken. He recalls: 'It was difficult to produce a painting without a focal point that would be visually stimulating. This one was more about emotion than timber and sail-cloth. I painted a deliberately high horizon to give the impression of scale, with the anvil-hard rock face illuminated by a blast of light, leaden sky and towering waves advancing relentlessly westward.' In this commissioned painting, Steven endeavoured to recreate the emotion that a sailor inevitably feels when he sees Cape Horn for the first time.